Ice Fishing

By Laura Purdie Salas

Consultant:
Betty L. Lewis
Youth Activities Coordinator
Maine Department of Inland
Fisheries & Wildlife

CAPSTONE
HIGH-INTEREST
BOOKS

an imprint of Capstone Press
Mankato, Minnesota

Capstone High-Interest Books are published by Capstone Press
151 Good Counsel Drive, P.O. Box 669, Mankato, Minnesota 56002
http://www.capstone-press.com

Library of Congress Cataloging-in-Publication Data
Salas, Laura Purdie.
    Ice fishing/by Laura Purdie Salas.
    p. cm.—(The great outdoors)
    Includes bibliographical references and index (p. 48).
    Summary: Describes the history, equipment, techniques, conservation issues,
rules, and safety concerns related to the sport of ice fishing.
    ISBN 0-7368-1056-0
    1. Ice Fishing—Juvenile literature. [1. Ice fishing. 2. Fishing.] I. Title. II. Series.
SH455.45 .S23 2002
799.1'22—dc21   2001002858

Editorial Credits
Carrie Braulick, editor; Timothy Halldin, cover and interior designer; Katy Kudela,
    photo researcher

Photo Credits
Brian Parker/TOM STACK & ASSOCIATES, 40 (bottom)
Capstone Press/Gary Sundermeyer, cover (bottom left, bottom right), 4,
    9 (foreground), 12, 17 (foreground), 18, 22, 23, 24, 30, 32, 35, 38, 45
Comstock, Inc., 1, 9 (background), 17 (background)
John Gerlach/TOM STACK & ASSOCIATES, 10
Richard Hamilton Smith, cover (top right)
Rob and Ann Simpson, 6, 41 (bottom), 42 (top)
Thomas Kitchin/TOM STACK & ASSOCIATES, 41 (top)
Unicorn Stock Photos/Ronald E. Partis, 14, 26; Aneal Vohra, 21
Visuals Unlimited/John Sohlden, 36; Rob and Ann Simpson, 40 (top); Patrice Ceisel,
    42 (bottom)

1 2 3 4 5 6 07 06 05 04 03 02

5519 6361

Table of Contents

CHAPTER 1

Ice Fishing

Ice fishing is a popular winter activity in Canada and the northern United States. People fish on frozen rivers, lakes, and ponds. They cut holes through the ice to catch fish.

History of Ice Fishing

People have fished through the ice for thousands of years. Many early ice fishers caught fish to survive. They needed the fish for food during the long northern winters. More than 3,000 years ago, people living in Alaska and Canada made ice fishing spears. They made the spears from materials such as animal bone or wood. They cut holes

Ice fishing is a popular sport in Canada and the northern United States.

Modern equipment makes ice fishing easier than it was in the past.

in shallow areas of frozen water. The ice fishers then used the spears to pierce fish that swam underneath the holes.

Early ice fishers also used hooks and line. They made the hooks from materials such as animal bone or rock. They attached a hook to a horsehair or silk line. They then attached bait to the hook and placed the line in the water. The ice fishers waited for a fish to eat the bait and become caught on the hook. They then pulled up the line to bring the fish out of the water.

Modern Ice Fishing

In the 1950s, ice fishing became popular as a recreational activity in North America. It was no longer necessary for people's survival. But people still enjoyed ice fishing and eating the fish that they caught.

Modern equipment made the activity easier than it had been in the past. Power augers allowed ice fishers to cut through the ice. Snowmobiles helped ice fishers travel onto the ice. Ice fishers also began to use modern rods and reels specially made for ice fishing.

Today, people ice fish for a variety of reasons. Many ice fishers enjoy spending time outdoors. People also may ice fish to spend time with others. Some ice fishers enjoy the challenge of trying to catch a "trophy" fish. These fish usually are much larger than other fish of the same kind.

Ice Fishing Locations

People can ice fish in a variety of freshwater areas such as lakes, ponds, streams, and rivers. Freshwater contains little salt. Seas and oceans contain salt water. Ice fishers do not fish in seas and oceans because they usually do not freeze.

North Americans mainly ice fish in Canada and the far northern areas of the United States. Water sources in some states sometimes have enough ice for a short ice fishing season. These states include Missouri, Virginia, Arizona, and New Mexico. The water that freezes in these areas is located at high elevations.

Certain areas are more popular ice fishing locations than others. The northeastern United States is a popular ice fishing area. The activity also is common in Minnesota, Wisconsin, and in the Great Lakes region near Michigan. Many people ice fish in the eastern Canadian provinces of Quebec and Newfoundland.

Italian Style Walleye

Ingredients:
6 walleye fillets
15-ounce (425-gram) can tomato
    sauce
2 teaspoons (10 mL) dried parsley
1 teaspoon (5 mL) Italian seasoning
½ teaspoon (2 mL) dried basil
¼ teaspoon (1 mL) salt
⅛ teaspoon (.5 mL) pepper
4 ounces (113 grams) shredded
    mozzarella cheese

Equipment:
Cooking spray
9- by 13-inch (23- by
    33-centimeter) cake pan
Medium bowl
Mixing spoon
Metal spatula
Fork

1. Lightly coat cake pan with cooking spray.

2. Place walleye fillets in pan.

3. In bowl, mix the tomato sauce, parsley, Italian seasoning, basil, and salt and pepper together.

4. Pour the mixture over the fillets.

5. Bake uncovered at 350°F (175°C) for 15 minutes.

6. Turn fish over with metal spatula. Sprinkle cheese over the fish.

7. Bake 5 to 10 minutes more. Fish is done when it is hot in the center and it flakes easily when touched with a fork.

Serves: 4 to 6   *Children should have adult supervision.*

Types of Fish

North Americans can ice fish for a variety of fish species. Animals in a species share certain physical features.

Some people ice fish for panfish. These small fish include species such as bluegill, pumpkinseeds, white crappies, and yellow perch. Panfish often live in shallow lakes close to shore.

Ice fishers may try to catch fish species that are larger than panfish. These fish include pike, walleye, burbot, and salmon. Ice fishers also can fish for trout and bass. Larger fish species often live in lakes. But they also may live in streams and rivers.

Ice fishers sometimes catch pike.

CHAPTER 2

Equipment

Ice fishers must have a great deal of equipment. Many ice fishers use sleds to pull their gear across the ice. Ice fishers need rods, line, hooks, and bait. Many ice fishers use lures. These manufactured wood, metal, or plastic objects are designed to attract fish.

Jigging Rods

Ice fishers use jigging rods. These rods usually are made of fiberglass or graphite. These materials are lightweight and strong. Most jigging rods are between 2 and 3.5 feet (.6 and 1 meter) long. This length allows ice fishers to sit close to the hole.

Ice fishers may use sleds to haul their equipment across the ice.

Tip-ups have a flag that pops up when a fish puts pressure on the line.

Jigging rods have a reel or line winder attached to them. Both reels and line winders hold fishing line. But line winders do not have a drag system. A reel's drag system allows ice fishers to adjust the pressure on the line as a hooked fish swims. The pressure helps keep the hook in the fish's mouth.

Tip-Ups

Many ice fishers use wooden, metal, or plastic devices called tip-ups. Tip-ups allow ice fishers to leave their holes. Ice fishers do not need to hold onto a rod when they use tip-ups.

Tip-ups have a frame attached to a reel. The reel has line wound around it. Ice fishers place the frame over the hole. They attach their bait or lure to a hook at the end of the line. They then lower the line into the water.

The reel has a flag with a spring attached to it. The spring causes the flag to pop up when a fish puts pressure on the line. Ice fishers tug the line to set the hook after the flag pops up. This action pushes the hook into the fish's mouth. Ice fishers then use the reel to bring the fish out of the water.

Tip-ups allow ice fishers to fish in several locations at once. Some ice fishers spread tip-ups as much as 100 feet (30 meters) apart.

Bait and Lures

Ice fishers can use a variety of live bait. They often use minnows. These small fish usually are less than 2 inches (5 centimeters) long. Minnows can include a variety of fish such as smelt, shiners, or chub. Ice fishers also may use worms or salmon eggs as bait. Some ice fishers use small bluegill as bait to catch large fish.

Ice fishers also may use dead bait. The scent of dead bait can attract fish such as pike and salmon.

Some ice fishers even use food such as cake or raw oatmeal to attract fish. The cake and oatmeal absorb water and sink. Fish that smell the bait may eat it.

Ice fishers sometimes use lures. Lures imitate the vibration, color, scent, or movement of food that a fish would eat. Ice fishers often use shiny metal objects called spoons. Some ice fishers use jigging minnows. These lures move sideways when ice fishers lift them up and let them drop. They are designed to look like minnows that are trying to escape.

Ice fishers also may use jigs. These small lead or metal balls are painted to look like an insect's head. Ice fishers often use small jigs called teardrops. Teardrops come in a variety of shapes, colors, and styles. Swimming jigs move

Equipment

- Bait
- Bait bucket
- Compass
- Depth finder
- Drinking water
- First aid kit
- Hot drinks
- Ice chisel or auger
- Ice pick
- Jigging rod
- Lake map
- Leader
- Line winder
- Lures
- Pack boots
- Portable heater
- Sinkers
- Skimmer
- Tip-ups

Ice fishers use ice houses made from a variety of materials.

in a circle when ice fishers lift and drop them. They imitate dying minnows.

Ice fishers often add live bait to their lures. The combination of a lure and bait can help attract fish.

Ice Houses

Many ice fishers use ice houses to help them stay comfortable in cold weather. These shelters can be made from a variety of materials such as metal, wood, nylon, or plastic.

Portable ice houses usually are made of strong, lightweight materials such as nylon or polyethylene. These materials are resistant to wind and water. Ice fishers can fold up portable ice houses to move them easily. These houses usually fit no more than two people.

Some portable ice houses have a plastic or wooden floor and a metal frame. The floors have holes to fit over the holes in the ice.

Some ice fishers use permanent ice houses. Ice fishers usually use trailers attached to vehicles to bring these houses onto the ice. Permanent ice houses often are made of metal or wood. They may fit more than six people.

Clothing

Ice fishers need warm clothing. Most ice fishers dress in layers. They then can add or remove layers to stay comfortable.

The first clothing layer should keep ice fishers' skin dry. Ice fishers often use synthetic fabrics for this layer. Synthetic fabrics are made by people. Some ice fishers choose polyester or polypropylene. Polypropylene is a lightweight material that people use to make plastic products.

Ice fishers may choose wool for the middle layer. Wool keeps people warm even after it becomes wet.

The final clothing layer is called the shell. The shell should be resistant to wind and water. Gore-Tex is a popular material for this layer. It has a finish that resists moisture. Some ice fishers wear nylon snowmobile suits.

Ice fishers need other clothing items to stay warm. They need a hat and mittens or gloves. Most ice fishers wear pack boots. These boots have a waterproof rubber sole and a removable wool or felt liner. The top of pack boots usually is made of leather or synthetic materials.

Other Items

Ice fishers often carry other gear. They need hooks, leaders, and sinkers. Leaders are thin pieces of line. They usually are about 6 to 24 inches (15 to 61 centimeters) long. Ice fishers attach them to the end of their fishing line. Leaders are hard for fish to see. Fish that see the line may not take the bait or lure. Sinkers are small metal objects that keep bait near the water's bottom.

Some ice fishers use manual augers to make holes in the ice.

Ice fishers also need equipment to cut holes. They may use an ice chisel. This tool sometimes is called a spud. Ice chisels have a long handle and a sharp metal blade. They usually are about 4 feet (1.2 meters) long.

Ice fishers also can use manual or power augers to cut ice holes. Ice fishers operate manual augers by hand. Manual augers have a handle and metal blades. They usually are about

Ice Fishing Lures

Ice Fishing Bait

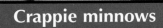

Crappie minnows

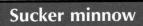

Sucker minnow

Fathead minnows

Waxworms

Many ice fishers bring snacks and warm drinks to help them stay warm.

3 feet (.9 meter) long. Ice fishers place the blades on the ice and turn the handle. This action causes the auger's blades to cut into the ice. Power augers have an engine that powers the blades.

Ice fishers need a skimmer to clear ice chips floating in holes. Skimmers have a handle and a scooper with small holes.

Many ice fishers use depth finders. These battery-powered electronic devices use sound waves to locate underwater objects. Depth finders also are called fish finders or sonar units. Depth finders have a screen. The screen shows the location of fish, the water's bottom, and the ice fisher's bait or lure.

Ice fishers often use heat sources to keep themselves warm. Most ice fishers use portable heaters inside their ice houses. Some permanent ice houses have built-in stoves. Outdoor ice fishers may have small heaters to keep their hands and feet warm. Heaters and stoves often are powered by fuels such as gas or propane.

Most ice fishers carry a compass and a map of their fishing area. These items can help prevent ice fishers from becoming lost.

Some ice fishers carry a small tool with a sharp point called an ice pick. Ice fishers who fall through the ice can use it to pull themselves out of the water.

Many ice fishers bring hot drinks in a thermos. They also may bring high-energy snacks such as beef jerky, chocolate bars, dried fruit, or peanuts.

CHAPTER 3

Skills and Techniques

Ice fishers must learn a variety of skills and make many decisions before they begin fishing. They must learn about the features and habits of different fish species. They need to decide where to cut holes. They also need to know what to do after a fish takes their bait or lure.

Locations
Ice fishers can look for fish in various areas. Fish often live in shallow areas of water. Panfish especially are common in these areas. Many fish live near weeds or structures such as logs or rocks. Some species commonly spend time in areas of deep water.

Ice fishers need to decide where to cut holes before they begin fishing.

Ice fishers can use several methods to choose a fishing location. Many ice fishers use depth finders or contour maps. These maps show the formation of a lake's bottom. Lines called contours show the water's depth in different locations. Some ice fishers look through clear ice to find an ideal fishing location. They may be able to see weedy areas or structures.

In deep lakes, ice fishers may use a bottom finder. These sinkers attach to the hook and line on a tip-up. Ice fishers drop the bottom finder to the water's bottom. They then lift the sinker out of the water and measure the line to find out the water's depth.

Ice fishers sometimes fish in uncrowded areas. Areas with many fishers often are noisy. The noise may frighten fish. These fish then may swim to other areas.

When to Fish

Ice fishers should learn the common feeding times of different fish species. Ice fishers sometimes catch more fish during feeding times. Walleye often feed just before sunrise and just after dark. Bluegill often feed in late afternoon.

Contour Map

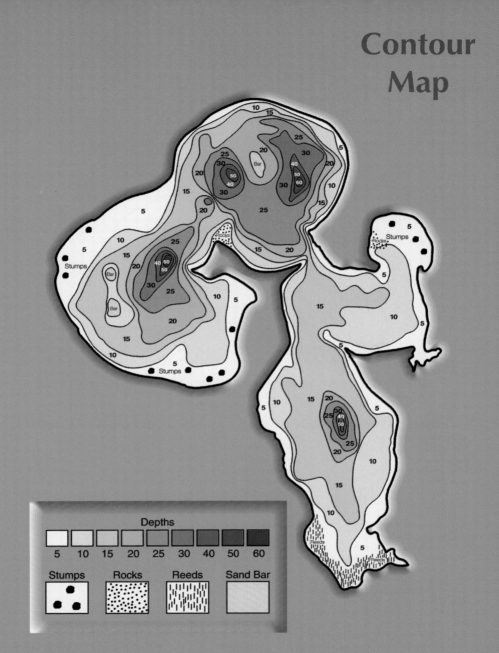

Ice fishers can use various jigging methods to catch fish.

Ice fishers also can use spawning times to decide when to fish. Fish lay eggs during these times. Some species feed more often than usual just before and after they spawn. Most fish spawn in spring. Ice fishers may try to catch spawning fish just before the ice begins to thaw.

Jigging Methods

Ice fishers often use a method called "jigging" to attract fish. They usually place the bait or lure about 18 inches (46 centimeters) from the water's bottom. They then gently move the rod upward and let the bait or lure settle. Ice fishers often repeat the movement several times to attract fish.

Ice fishers may modify their jigging techniques. The technique they choose may depend on the fish species or time of day. For example, ice fishers may forcefully lift the rod upward. This action may attract a fish species during times when it is less likely to feed. Ice fishers also may gently wiggle the bait or lure as they jig. This action sometimes attracts panfish. Ice fishers also can tap their bait on the water's bottom or jig more frequently than usual.

Landing a Fish

Ice fishers must bring the fish out of the water after it takes the bait or lure. This practice is called landing the fish.

Ice fishers follow several steps to land a fish. They first quickly snap their wrist upward to set the hook. Ice fishers then usually let the fish swim a few feet or meters. They may let a large fish swim until it becomes tired. Ice fishers then reel in the fish or lift the rod to bring the fish out of the water.

CHAPTER 4

Conservation

Responsible ice fishers take care of the environment. They follow regulations to protect fish populations and habitats. Habitats are the natural conditions and places in which fish live.

Licenses and Regulations

State and provincial government agencies set various ice fishing regulations. Regulations require that ice fishers buy fishing licenses when they reach a certain age. This age can vary from about 12 to 16.

Government agencies also set limits. Limits regulate the number of fish a person can catch and take home in one day. These limits vary according to the species and time of year.

Regulations may require that ice fishers release fish.

Some ice fishing regulations limit the number of tip-ups and jigging rods people can use. For example, ice fishers may only be allowed to use five tip-ups at a time.

Government agencies also set minimum sizes. Fish smaller than the minimum size must be released. This law helps make sure that fish grow old enough to spawn.

Releasing Fish

Ice fishers should release fish that they do not plan to keep. They should handle these fish gently to prevent injuries to the fish.

Ice fishers should try to keep a fish in the water as they release it. Fish that are removed from the water cannot receive oxygen through their gills. These openings are along a fish's sides. The fish then may die.

Protecting Water Sources

Some water sources are becoming polluted. Wastes from factories and chemicals used in farming can pollute water sources. Pollutants can enter the bodies of fish. Fish with pollutants in them can become sick or die.

Some regulations limit the number of lines ice fishers can have in the water.

Ice fishers should try to prevent pollution and damage to water sources. They should leave their fishing area as they found it. Responsible fishers place trash in a trash can or take it home with them.

Ice fishers should enter and exit the water on level ground. Ice fishers who enter and exit the water on steep slopes may cause soil erosion. Soil that wears away in steep areas can easily enter water sources. Water areas with too much soil can damage places where fish spawn.

CHAPTER 5

Safety

Ice fishers must be careful on the ice. Ice of any thickness can have weak spots. Ice fishers must learn the ice thickness in their fishing location. Many people fish with a partner. Partners can help one another in dangerous situations.

Ice Thickness

The safety of a frozen water area depends on how much weight it needs to support. People usually can walk safely on ice that is at least 5 inches (13 centimeters) thick. Ice that is about 8 to 12 inches (20 to 30 centimeters) thick usually can support a car or pick-up truck.

Ice fishers should look for signs that ice is unsafe. Crunchy ice or ice with a soft top layer

Ice fishers should make sure ice is safe before they travel onto it.

Ice fishers should stay away from areas of thin ice.

often is weak. Weak ice also may be gray-black instead of clear. People sometimes place signs where weak ice areas are located. These signs help warn others of dangerous conditions. Ice on rivers and streams usually is about 15 percent weaker than ice on other water areas. The currents prevent thick ice from forming.

Hypothermia and Frostbite

Ice fishers need to stay warm. Ice fishers who become too cold can get hypothermia. This condition occurs when a person's body temperature becomes too low. Signs of hypothermia include shivering, slurred speech, and confusion. Hypothermia may cause death.

Ice fishers also can get frostbite. This condition occurs when skin freezes. Frostbitten skin often becomes white and waxy. The condition can cause permanent damage to skin.

Ice House Safety

Gas and propane heaters give off a poisonous gas called carbon monoxide. This gas is colorless and odorless. People inside an ice house who breathe too much of the gas can get carbon monoxide poisoning. This condition can cause headaches, sleepiness, and confusion. It may cause death. Ice houses should have at least two small openings. The gas then can escape through these holes.

Responsible ice fishers enjoy their activity while staying safe. They prevent dangerous situations. They share their knowledge with others. These ice fishers help keep the activity safe for other participants in the sport.

Northern Pike

Description: Northern pike are dark bronze. They are long and slim. Their tail and fins are red. Northern pike have rows of white and yellow spots along their sides. Scales cover their cheeks and the upper half of their gill covers. Northern pike have sharp teeth. They usually weigh about 4 pounds (1.8 kilograms). But many pike weigh more than 10 pounds (4.5 kilograms).

Habitat: shallow, weedy areas; near structures

Food: other fish, frogs, ducklings

Bait and lures: large minnows, dead bait, bladebaits, spoons, jigs

Walleye

Description: Walleye vary in color. They may be various shades of yellow, yellow-red, or yellow-blue. Walleye have small spots above their white underside. They have large eyes. Walleye usually weigh about 3 to 10 pounds (1.4 to 4.5 kilograms).

Habitat: open areas in large lakes; cold, deep water near drop-offs and weeds in lakes

Food: minnows, small fish

Bait and lures: nightcrawlers, minnows, deep diving spoons

Black Crappies

Description: Black crappies are silver-green with black spots. Black crappies have one dorsal fin. Dorsal fins are located on a fish's back. Black crappies have gill covers with sharp spines. They usually weigh about 4 pounds (1.8 kilograms).

Habitat: weedy and rocky areas

Food: small fish, insects, worms

Bait and lures: minnows, beetlespins

Yellow Perch

Description: Yellow perch can be various shades of green, yellow, or gray. They have dark vertical bars on their sides. Their lower fins are orange-yellow. They usually weigh about 2 pounds (.9 kilogram).

Habitat: open areas in lakes; weedy areas

Food: minnows, insects, worms

Bait and lures: minnows, worms, jigs

Pumpkinseed

Description: Pumpkinseed are blue-green to gray. They have a red-orange belly and a red-orange ear spot. They have dark blue upper gill covers. Pumpkinseed have one dorsal fin. This fin has pointed edges in the front and becomes rounded toward the rear. Pumpkinseed usually weigh less than 2 pounds (.9 kilogram).

Habitat: shallow, weedy areas in lakes

Food: small, young insects

Bait and lures: waxworms

White Bass

Description: White bass are silver-white with horizontal dark stripes. White bass have two dorsal fins. White bass usually weigh about .5 pound (.2 kilogram).

Habitat: near rocky areas; open areas in lakes

Food: insects, minnows, small fish, worms, small shelled animals

Bait and lures: minnows, jigs, spoons

Words to Know

carbon monoxide (KAR-buhn muh-NOK-side)—a colorless, odorless gas; carbon monoxide is poisonous to people.

contour (KON-toor)—a line on a map that shows the elevation of an area

fiberglass (FYE-bur-glass)—a strong, lightweight material made from thin threads of glass

frostbite (FRAWST-bite)—a condition that occurs when cold temperatures freeze skin

habitat (HAB-uh-tat)—the places and natural conditions in which a plant or animal lives

hypothermia (hye-puh-THUR-mee-uh)—a condition that occurs when a person's body temperature becomes too low

polypropylene (pah-lee-PROH-puh-leen)—a lightweight material used to make plastic products

spawn (SPAWN)—to lay a large number of eggs; fish such as salmon spawn.

To Learn More

Fitzgerald, Ron. *Essential Fishing for Teens.* Outdoor Life. New York: Children's Press, 2000.

Gruenwald, Tom. *Modern Methods of Ice Fishing.* The Freshwater Angler. Minnetonka, Minn.: Creative Publishing, 1999.

Hopkins, Ellen. *Freshwater Fishing.* The Great Outdoors. Mankato, Minn.: Capstone High-Interest Books, 2002.

You also can read about ice fishing in magazines such as *In-Fisherman* and *Field & Stream.*

Useful Addresses

American Sportfishing Association
1033 North Fairfax Street
Suite 200
Alexandria, VA 22314

Canadian Wildlife Service
Environment Canada
Ottawa, ON K1A 0H3
Canada

U.S. Fish and Wildlife Service
4401 North Fairfax Drive
Arlington, VA 22203

Internet Sites

Canadian Wildlife Service
http://www.cws-scf.ec.gc.ca/cwshom_e.html

Ice Fishing Home
http://www.icefishinghome.com

Panfishing Tackle and Techniques
http://ngp.ngpc.state.ne.us/fish/tacktech.html

Save Yourself!—Make a Set of Ice Rescue Claws
http://www.dnr.state.mn.us/information_and_
    education/ice_safety/iceclaws.html

U.S. Fish & Wildlife Service
http://www.fws.gov

Index